Day Rudimental Solos

By Paul Smith

AF887285

About the Solos

As the title suggests, the five solos in this collection were written in the span of one day. While never the intent, they developed quickly as they took their final form.

For Rolls—Written in a constant meter, this solo includes a variety of roll types throughout.

Cross Phase—This solo uses triplets, sextuplets and varying tempos to create its mood.

Left Ha!—Focusing primarily on the left hand, this solo utilizes a variety of meters and an extremely soft ending to create a unique challenge.

March Tax Fast—Using two contrasting tempos, this straightforward march is the desired goal.

Pepper 4-3—Focusing on changing meters, this solo combines various sections from the other solos to create a unique conclusion.

Table of Contents

Alfred's
PERCUSSION
PERFORMANCE SERIES

Alfred

For Rolls

Paul Smith

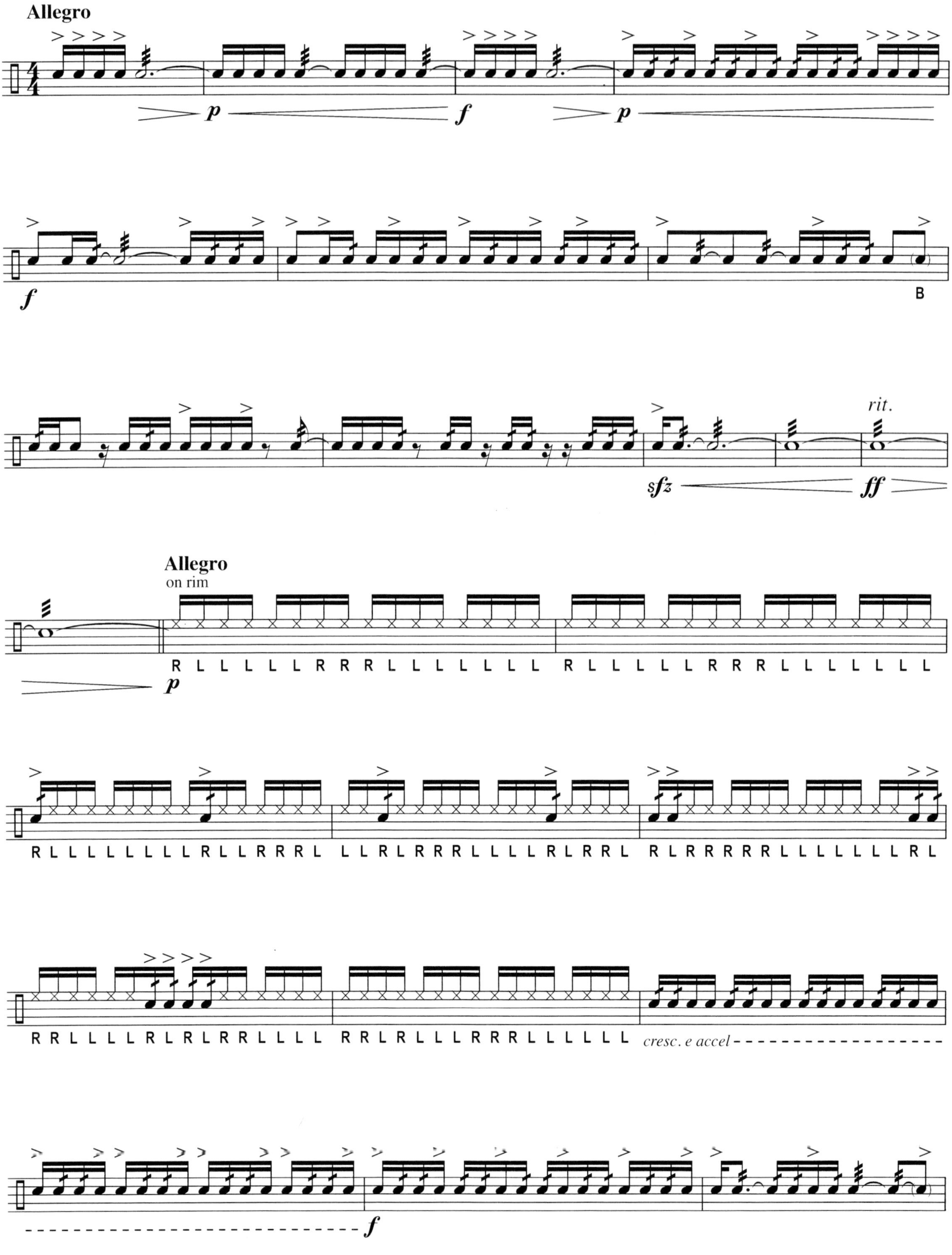

p f p
R R L L R R L L R R L L R R L L
rit.
A tempo
R R L L R R L L R R L L B R
f R R R R R R R L R R R R R R L R R R
sfz f
R R R R
p
f
R R R
p f p f
R R
p f p
f
p f p f
p < f p < f
> p < f
R
mf
B R B R
p
f
mf
ff

Cross Phase

Paul Smith

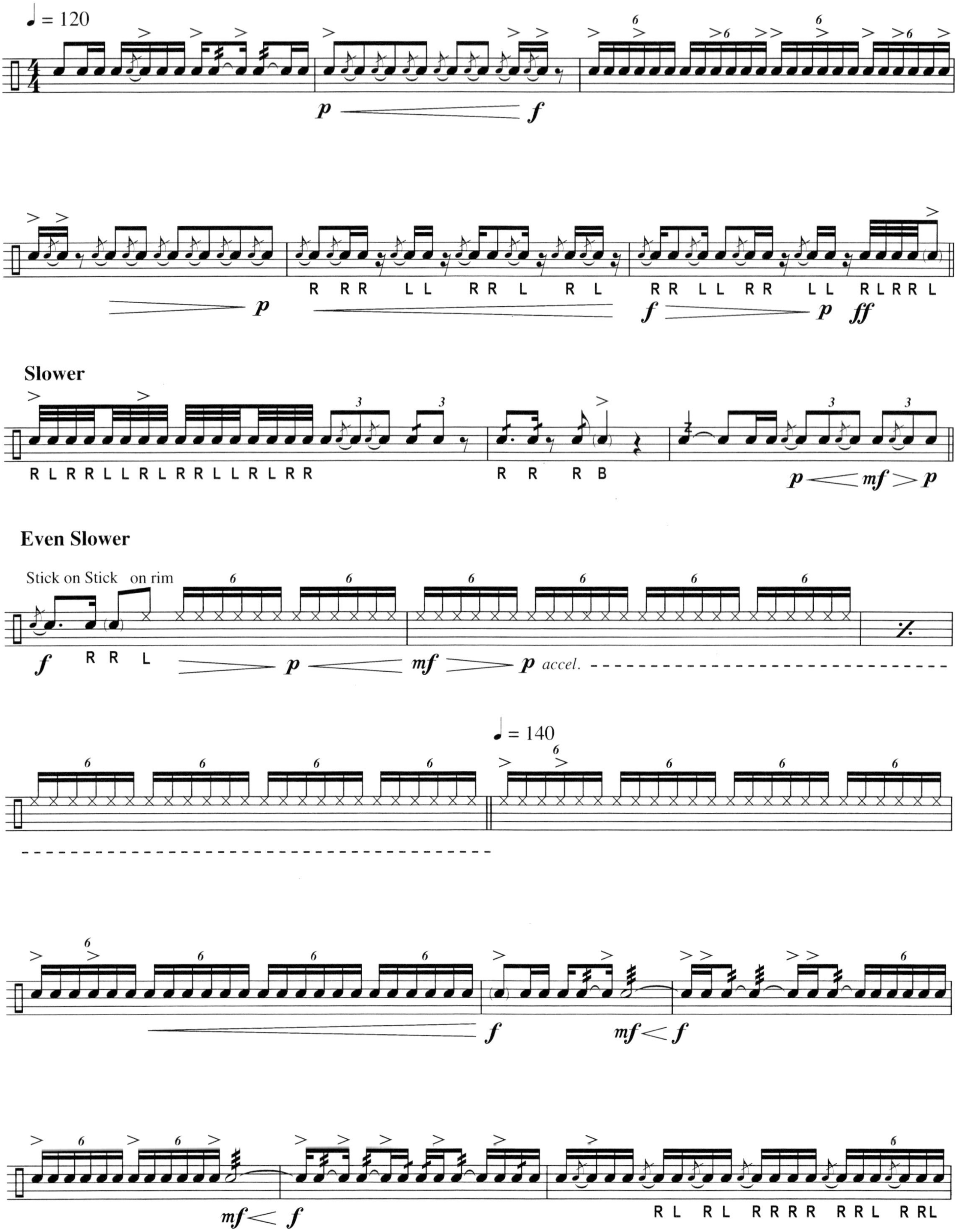

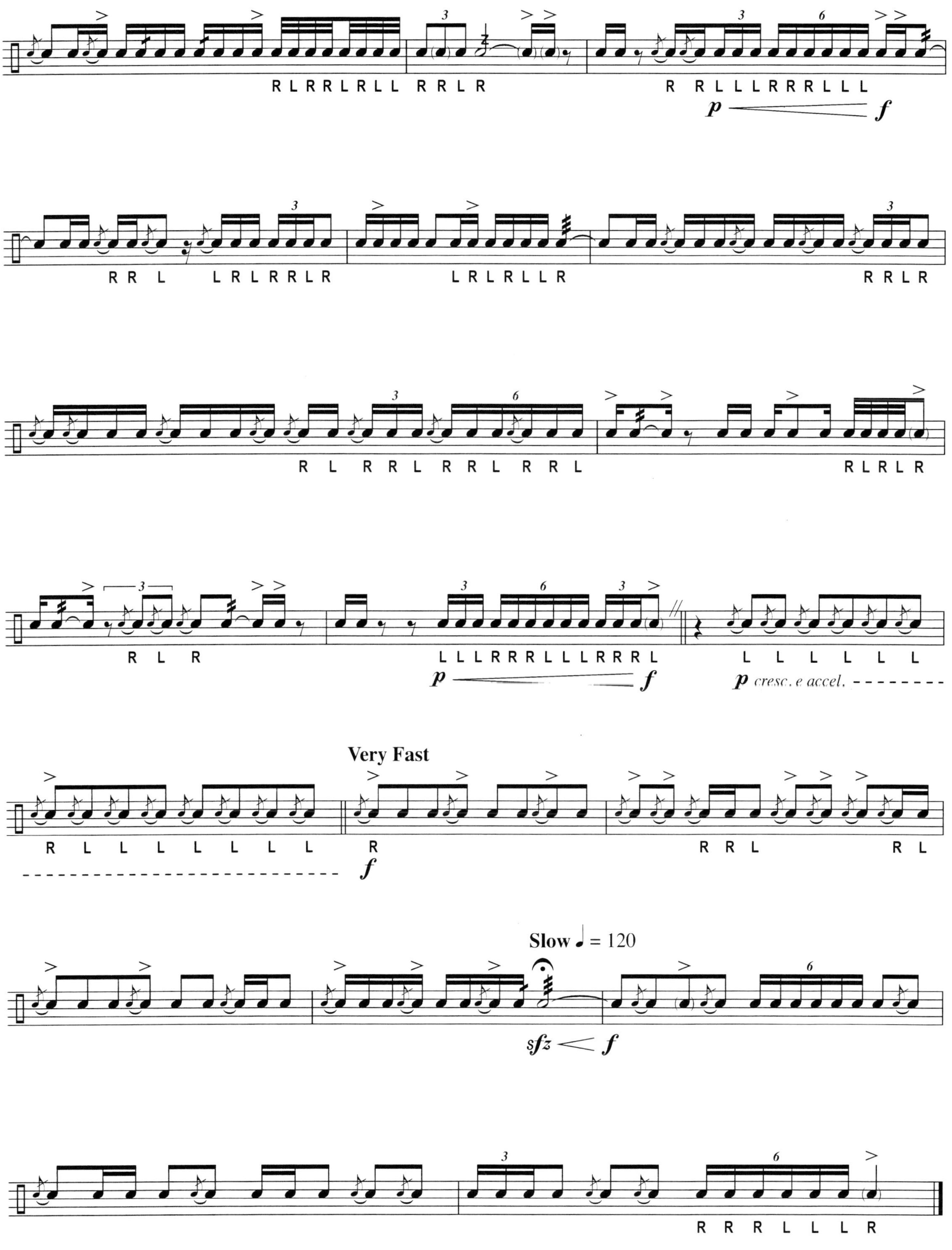
R L R R L R L L R R L R
R R L L L R R R L L L
p f
R R L L R L R R L R
L R L R L L R
R R L R
R L R R L R R L R R L
R L R L R
R L R
L L L R R R L L L R R R L
p f
L L L L L L
p cresc. e accel.
Very Fast
R L L L L L L L
R
f
R R L R L
Slow ♩ = 120
sfz f
R R R L L L R

Left Ha!

Paul Smith

Stick on Stick in Air
dim. e accel. al fine

March Tax Fast

Paul Smith

RRL RRL RRL R L
LRLL
RRRLLL RRRLLLRLR
RRL R
RR LL
B
♩ = 112
RRL
♩ = 140
♩ = 112
RRL R

Pepper 4-3

Paul Smith

mp
f
R L R R RR LL RR
R
R L L L L
L L L L
mp
R R L R L
f
L L
RRL R L
p
RRL RRLRLR
ff
mf
ff
sfz
R R
mf
p
f
sfz
ff